The Ghosts of Anne & Sylvia

D1521072

The Ghosts of Anne & Sylvia

Amber LaParne & Jasmine Paul

iUniverse, Inc.
New York Bloomington Shanghai

The Ghosts of Anne & Sylvia

iUniverse books may be ordered through booksellers or by contacting:

iUniverse
1663 Liberty Drive
Bloomington, IN 47403
www.iuniverse.com
1-800-Authors (1-800-288-4677)

Because of the dynamic nature of the Internet, any Web addresses or links contained in this book may have changed since publication and may no longer be valid.

ISBN: 978-0-595-51226-3 (pbk)
ISBN: 978-0-595-61810-1 (ebk)

Printed in the United States of America

For the young women at Havermale High School,
who continue to inspire us much more than they can ever know.

Authors' Note

For the past few years we have had the privilege of working with some wonderful young students from Havermale High School in Spokane, Washington. The opportunity to participate in Havermale's yearly writer's workshop has done so much for us and the experience truly inspired this book of poetry. Every young woman in our poetry seminar poured her story out, without hesitation, and should be commended on the bravery that takes.

We had long been avid poetry fans, each writing, reading, speaking and participating separately in the world of poetry. We realized that we could come together and produce a collaborative work in order to share it with those individuals who had long been appreciative of our poetry.

As dedicated fans of Anne Sexton and Sylvia Plath, we both realized that our work shared very similar themes to those of the two women who so deeply inspired us. We saw also that our work complemented and strengthened each others. It was when compiling these poems into a book that the cadence, rhythm and thematic content began to blend in ways we had never seen in another collaborative work of poetry.

We hope that you enjoy the poems as this project has been a true labor of love.

for anne

they said *anne, flee on your donkey*
as you spooled through
their antiseptic corridors
dimly lit castles
of Lysol and lithium

I fell into your world
of doctors and heroes
transformations isolation
I decoded the language of our dark cure,
of our dancing partner
with his slippery seductive tongue

your poems built a room inside my chest
a safe haven
for lunatics and fingernails
when life demanded a smile
and Doris Day

oh anne, anne
of the mayflies
anne of the cure
anne of the light extinguished

let me give you this gift. I will
take your donkey and flee
carry your ashes to mercy street

blessed and sprinkled
with words with reverence
with peace

in memory of Anne Sexton and all her terrible beauty

A.S.L.

narcissus

you great golden fool, I
look right at you, you know
we
look awfully similar, we
both have blood red poppies in our veins, we have
daddies so much the same

and you went and left, but left
your face
which is mine now, which
is mine

you took that ride in your red lipstick and small handed
oven-mitts, but left
your reflection
which is mine, which I eat
deep
the silver wash of mirrors and memories
we shared

and I am drowning now in you, which
is us
and I am trying to steer this thing
that we birthed
that was born too big for us to carry and I am
trying to steer this hearse
that carries

too much

for Sylvia, who knew better

J.P.

persephone beneath the blue glass

tell us again how
you were stolen, the sun's
only daughter

born lonely in the black hills
of San Joaquin
queen of the honey bees
        and orange blossom

tell us how the earth split
open and swallowed
you

how you ended up a wife
with a brand new Hoover, a pretty
lace apron
one boy on each hip

when other girls were sewing prom dresses

living your half life underground, nuclear
and swimming that
river of whiskey, still thirsty and nibbling
darvonvaliumpercoset
like the seeds of a pomegranate

and tarantula tequila
poured out even
like a sheet of blue glass

A.S.L.

trying to drown

thin in white dresses
we promised them everything
and ate what we thought were rocks, really
      hand shaped meats
with bits of weed root, you thought goldenrod
but I knew better

we knew that yelling in hot, small rooms
scarred the plaster
and you could feel the bites in the drywall when
I ran your fingers over them
like stretch marks
is what you said
and so you went to sleep, disgusted
and we dreamed of vomiting worms

in the morning we promised again
with words cold and definite
we promised something slick
with antiseptic
ripe with health
it was your fault, I think
no, yours

but you became meek, no you
and whispered

just how the ocean would hold you
      when you were trying to drown

J.P

virginia dreams softly

let us speak as sisters do, foreheads
touching
on the sun dried sheet

as the light stumbles evening into
its fine wide hands
there is no universe, but this bed

Soon enough it will be time for the clink of bone china
Spoons like tiny silver chains
The best sugar and polite conversation
little bits of cyanide dissolving in a fine oolong.

Oh the dreadful weight of teacups!

Give me back my milky way
Strewn with organza stars and the silent whisper of our eyelashes
A galaxy without drawing rooms or husbands,
Filled with the warm staccato of our fingertips speaking in brail.

I watch you across the table and dream of
That first shock of cold water
Reeds like a burst of spring
Whispering the secret language of river stones.

A.S.L.

the kitchen table

Madeline said that she's tired of surviving
where hurt collapses around hurt and saran wraps like
layered spit
she spoke of this in the kitchen over
hot mugs of orange tea

Madeline said her mother was a geisha with small hands
that all her pain felt like those snapshots
of Saigon
when people filed their nails to knives
dug into the plane wheels
trying to get out

J.P.

the cure

you are red Shanghai silk, merlot
spilled careless
a martini olive with an aged
gorgonzola center

let's walk in the jazz of this downtown, your hand
through mine
let's blow girl kisses
at the women on corners
who clutch their purses
closer

we are contagion and lovely now

with the traffic sounds like Miles Davis
kind of blue, this rain
is his staccato

let's blow loose on pavement, girl
Gene Kelly's
and let the vodka run through us
like a cure

A.S.L.

silence

We walked awhile through Angelene sprawl, urban rust
bright oranges you stirred to foam about your knees
My fingers were bleeding. This I remember,
the vague taste of something
I had been clawing

You do not know how quiet I've been
My convulsed bird tongue
caught
tightly livered eyes glue in my cheeks
The zoo of my lips spits rustling only

Still we walked awhile
and passers-by became generations, then horses
and we rode further apart
I shrugged a thousand cool arcs
with each of your silences, was chafed
with every stingy exhale
I swear I saw empty vowels tearing at your hair

You do not know how silent I've been, clipped words
winged rot in the sun

We rode awhile
until the horses grew steel and magazines
until the height of first class economy
by then
it was your scent I listened for
the call of your fist cupping a match
the different speeches behind your belt buckles,
one for brown and two for black

You do not know how quiet I've been, waiting
for the ground again

To scrape my language from beneath your shoes, those
laced sayings you do not undo
You keep moving

You bring me a drink. I cannot trust it.
It reeks of small, pet cages
Charlie Chaplin's mustache
a broken radio, ownerless
a little cupboard
Quietly miniscule your dialogue,
a peeled young rabbit

This journey is long, a silence
a border through my tongue

J.P.

my doppelganger

I am headed underground
to the cool still blue silence
to those layers of glass
finely ground sugar under my belly
a slow sigh of black water.

Some nights it bubbles like champagne
Other nights it is thick sticky molasses
Intoxicating and inescapable

Filling up my chest and settling in
As if to say
    Old friend it has been too long

Underground
has the taste of licorice and aspirin
It feels like cheap hospital sheets and gin
Gulped warm out of a stolen cup

Underground
is where Judas hid his thirty pieces of silver
before he stepped off the platform on the L-train.

Underground
The years of vicious thoughts
Begin to manifest themselves
On the war zone of this body.

A.S.L.

fool for hunger

I am a fool for hunger
the forest floor in my mouth
I conjured you, you
grew green and reedy
you leapt greedy from my throat

I am a fool for hunger, you
have strong milk
inside you, the sweet milk of
long fallow earth
I am a fool in this wood

history burned us over and over
and still you rose, history
burned us over and over, still
you grow

I recall your memories, often
fingered smooth grooves
my hands deep in pulp rings
palm to lips, I
cannot feed
your breadth spreads, I breathe
through my eyes

I remember everything
each knotted wooden sheet
you have white wet memory inside you
a dark bird's hovel, an unwritten novel
paper thin, weak

I am a fool beneath your branches shrug
razored speech pieces
dirty cut mouth dispersed

to sand, you have
Sequoia inside you
or nothing

I remember this hunger
remember you have
leaving inside you
each wintry change and fall
rooted deep, your wood in me
and I don't recall my breaking

J.P.

monday

The shades of your room
Glow wheat colored
An opaque diffusion of morning,
Elusive sunbeams
Slipping
Through the cracks between fabric and glass.

Let me trace
The path between your shoulder blades
With sleepy dawn kisses
Run my palms
Through the soft down of your thighs

Hold me
Back against chest
Lips
Against neck
We'll let the silence fill us like a prayer
Among the creaks
Of cats and coffee makers,
Alarm clocks and car engines,
Before the slow grind of everyday
We have this silence:

A benediction
Of wheat colored sun.

A.S.L.

panther's tale

I have paced
some German's panther
caged, counting bars
lapping fitful in the always night
while you danced on the rubble
left by old wars in old places

this is how I say
    that you've been gone

I remain kept, your face a keeper
its snare of brightness, a lurid lamp
occasionally bobs, a bit of flesh
I remember tasting

this is how I say
    that I was starving

I have circled my bed
three times each full moon
with feline grace, allowing my ears rise
for the jangle of keys
when you will lay down with me

this is how I say that I was waiting

there are voices in the evening, did you know
there are voices
that hold my breath, caress my flank
milk wet from the green of my eyes
there are a thousand tastes in breezes
I believed in you dreamt everything

this is how I say
        I was lonely

here I stretch, purr
I sense your inching close, so weary now
of the world
        (the wall feels soft to brush against)
that is your shadow I smell
        (these intricate weaves in the stone I walk on)
that is your hand I feel
        (your words full of locks I have no use for)

not a thing has changed
just the light in your face
has emptied

J.P.

sylvia

We are made of earth, constantly
Evolving to external pressure
Reshaping the lines of our bodies and our minds
Volcanic
Disruptive
Sensitive to subtle magnetic waves

Sylvia
You and I are made of dark stones
    Brittle obsidian
      Delicate jet
        Rare onyx black as the sky without a moon.

sharp edged, beautiful
      And easily
    Broken.

A.S.L.

wax giant, can you

Wax giant, can you sit
in the sun? My mother
dresses game. Can you spit
into the fire like my
whiskey licking uncles

Let me carve you a chair
smooth with deer skin
sloped boned seat whittled even
horny thorned
a crown for your ass
You waxy bastard eat deep this lie
meat buttered hot with spices, saliva
My family is silent

They don't know you
in their honest charade of furs, guns
accent sour curses. Could easy kill
with welfare grins, grunts
hot like Fourth of July

Big boy sit outside
warm your belly melt awhile
as we stumble in the Northern cottage
pintos boiled in bacon fat
Make the most of the night and
hang high your hat

My mother lisps her record voice
teeth shellacked
Marry no hunter's son, girl
and marry fast

J.P.

i slip

so quiet so sweet so soft
waiting
like a cracking
gaping fault line
waiting
like a weeping
whistling heart valve

waiting for your face to fall
for kindness to leak
out toward morning
for nothing
but the aftermath of your scent
and the stale trace
of evening

I slip each time
like the one before
with trust a beacon
lying suspended, low
and constant
in a sky, that rises
and falls with each passing wave

I would
maroon myself
broken
by the jagged shore

give me your lies, your sweet
untamed
unmentionable moonbeams
give me regret
with that flat and salty taste

A.S.L.

proof

My jury mouth ceases session, tongue
gavel real stretches to wood
There is no proof your eyes
have seen every move, nor proof
you have seen nothing

I approach you fatigued
seeking Vietnam, a DMZ
the atrocity of any city
to persecute that mute white
skin shielding your blood

There is no proof
that your heart hides jungles
ripe with corpses
Nor proof your heart conceals pits and coffins

You counter deaf, sullen
wipe grease from the stove top
fold your black socks
smooth the sheets perfectly

Your malignancy muscles through rooms
I cannot sleep in
Your motives motions secrecy
barbed flesh eaters
tumble about you like rabid puppies

There is no proof
you bled a woman's home
drained her fields
salted her earth
Nor proof your eyes are stone

or the weapons you wield
are fresh with hurt

I am the witness, the wire
you leak across
Leaving violent orders
in the clean creases of pants
in the freshly scrubbed bath

I am the witness with my jury mouth
my jury mouth
my throat tight with bones
those little deaths I swallowed
to understand you

If you are not guilty
I will speak until you are

J.P.

women who reject the moon

Matala
    off the coast of Southern Crete
wind comes in a warm rush from the Northern shore
    of Africa
fluttering among hunched women in black
with skin like fine, wrinkled
rice paper

In Crete
    the sun saturates worn limestone embattlements
She wears blue
scorching the air around her
shimmering straight white back
the gliding click of her walk
the long corn silk curl of her hair

At noon
church bells sound
with a ring like pewter
and morning
Brown children wander the worn stones of marketplace
slivers of silver laughter peal
almond eyes flashing
begging for a tourists picture or skin
off the wooden yogurt barrels

In Crete
    even the poor are beautiful

She wants to take a Greek lover
with warm breath
and calloused hands

She wants to count his eyelashes and forget
her American mediocrity

In Crete
　　　men and hours are counted in stars

One night she drinks hot lemonade
with a stranger
he offers her the island
bound in linen curtains
She would be a waitress
flirting innocent with Greek men
blonde women mean business in the land of olives and dark musk

In Crete
　　　opportunity has a sound like the Aegean

She will return
back to American bricks, only her
shadow remains
naked and dancing on the roof of a Greek hotel
exchanging love songs with the starlight

In the suburban days of her life
she'll never out run a loud rushing
grind in her eardrums

Regret is the sound of dreams gone lukewarm, the sound
of the Aegean

A.S.L.

one girl's winter

The Reservation held in winter, its crusts of brown
easy tipped with snow
found us snorting in the closest cold, stamping our boots
pink faced ponies
English books wedged between elbows and layers of clothing

What was frozen no longer ached with scanty green
we moved, muffled in wool
and you eased from boy to boy
notepad melting on the sidewalk
coat open
the curve of your new breasts full
rising beneath the softest cotton

In your too tight Levis, your smoky snarl
made me forget you were thirteen
Your sex rolled before you, ticking
like a bomb
You found your heat
not in the games of girls
rolling balls down icy streets, nor
in the damp whispers we shared over sugar
I watched the sway of your hips, listened
the coarseness of your laugh, heard
the reserved mouth men-children
whisper husky accent

Near campfires in the cool, crisp beer
frothed your upper lip
They came towards you
quiet as deer
You took those Native boys
their muscled stomachs

severe as horses hooves
under your tongue

How it must have felt
to knot their black braids around your fists
corral their bruised lips
in your angry paleness
and slide with the ice you had
slipped into sex on
and turn towards any distance
and ride so many horses
to the arms of any house that pulsed with life
that would take you in defiant

You would ease into my room
deep midnights shrouding your face
the musk of just mingled bodies on your neck
I curled in my flannel nightgown
you undressed yourself, blowing
smoke out my window
You brought with you the feel of
frostbitten leaves pressed
into lower backs
and terrible freedom

You would thaw beneath my sheets
voice slowing, breathing alcohol
and mint on my cheek
Exhales would bring the parade of your father's faults
his nomad hands
and steel blue eyes
that blinked beatings

In the morning, cornflakes
glued to your chin and sleep

making your eyes young
I wondered
which hour would be the line
you whirled across
and into the days womanhood
I wondered what line
would become a country's border
when we would no longer
be girls together

J.P.

delicate

All your pink dreams come fluttering
Down the slope of your new breasts,
the swell of your belly not quite a moon yet
soon it will be ripe;
full like the curve of a wave at it's perfect crest
aching for the tug and pull of tides and lips
sleepless and glowing,

delicate
like the first shell put to your child's ear carrying salt and seabirds in
    its coils,
delicate
starfish and purple urchins dancing in a rocky tide pool.

sail on down this marsh river
anchored to the mooring of your own skin
sail into this clear night
where each star has the shape of your mouth.

A.S.L.

joseph, i didn't

Joseph, I didn't
know you'd tire this way
the pages of novels stained
nicotine thumbed
how you breathe the breath of nuns
in your sterile room your
bed a fresh grave dug
head lowered
even your lovemaking is flowered
with church and isolation

Joseph, this light
grows cold you read religious
text, romantic trash, feeding
a man starving in his mother's kitchen
too much to you, the bread
you dip in milk at one a.m.
thrown to the wall with anger
at the frayed rag rug

Joseph, I never
knew the woman you love
nor heard her curse, words
that took her south
I never touched her hand or drank
her face
I never smoothed the air
from her great paled shout

Joseph, I didn't know she begged
    fly away from your stale bed

those gray sheets
damp with doubt

I didn't know she took your tongue
when you gave your mouth

J.P.

women who sing with chocolate in their throats

satin tumbling, fumbling
in the corners of your mouth
you are a stained cherry, a mahogany
drop of honey
in your throat, billie
the notes are a slippery shade of chocolate

when you sing
I can feel the poppy in your veins, moving
like slow silk
when you sing
I hear hollow footsteps on a brothel floor
young women in loose, aging bodies
long hallways with sharp corners, thin walls
and too many doors

was there music when you pawned your body, were there
saxophones purring
between your thighs
was it sex? was it jazz?

teach me how to fall in love
without apology how to
take a man's heart
and break it into pieces with a kiss

when you sing
I am surrounded by an ocean of white faces
a haze of cheap whiskey and smoke
I am stranded in the glare of a spotlight
when you sing
I see the harvest of georgia's strange fruit
strong black backs bloodied

graceful wrists bound and blowtorched
fine boned feet fluttering like paper in the wind

Ms. Holiday
you are broken and beautiful
a bright comet burning up our atmosphere
as you roll around your songs like candy
Ms. Holiday
you carried out your life
with a certain kind of style
a hint of burnt coffee
an unerring southern grace
and the clinging scent of gardenias

A.S.L.

metamorphosis

I could have said the Joshua trees
did it, made me take
your mouth to my own and your tongue
cool silver jewelry
at the base of my throat

it was the desert and the sight
of twisted rock and road sign
    one sign blank without your word
one turn into a town it
could have been anywhere
and my smile was pained as if
    the world had just begun with a break of stale rock
    and shed scales
    and you sliding ripe
wet around my bare feet

your heart could have been anywhere
except the desert made it then
and the trees made your words

and I did squint to find you
    white against a rock
    green against the flower
    black against the sky that night
but I swore I saw you
then I swore to have you
my changeling sand dune everything

I will call you back again

I will call you back again
when the air spins back to white shale dust

when sailors roam cactus canyons
    when the flood drinks Arizona

I will call you back again
when gulls carry sand and dip
like white balloons
into sunsets

I will call you back
with a serpentine hiss and many knives
    in my deep pockets

J.P.

may is when the fish bite

May is when the fish bite
I feel amphibian, with my neoprene waders
the sway of the line
popping silk wire flies on the river.

The trout know,
they play my game
running the yellow leader only to spit
and splash sunspots.

A.S.L.

swimming the length

I found predators
in hundreds
on travels that sped me aching
in trains, burning fields
with paid for distance
between my legs

they met me at the station

several steps ahead, sharing eyes
pacing and pickpocket hands
slim hipped
coarseness revealed in sex

I have seen the sluggish mud of Tennessee
eaten
catfish on the deck of a southern beast's mansion
while he pinched tobacco for his pipe
and set loose his hounds on rabbits

the whiskey drinker in Pennsylvania
and my fat thirst for him
his brow wrinkled with meat
tongue lapping loud, neck
wreathed in ribbons of tendon
how he won

they share the flesh propelling me, they
split the fist come down on me
cagey men, deep
trapping pits
after a storm
I cannot swim the length of a man's body safely

butterfly crawl on a lion's back
a slaughter of pigs at his feet

there have been many, slow
dances in carnivorous circles
their manes golden with the fire
I stoke in my head

J.P.

blue spanish dress

I swear you are my last mistake
a throbbing shade of red
in a sea of gray
and the lines of my suicide stretch
like fishing wire
across my forearms

you are the untainted corner of my womb
you are the throb in my comatose pulse
you are the blue Spanish dress
with the ripped hem

A.S.L

the last one

we will climb this
though I have no breath then
run fast down past children
clawing at mosquitoes and air

we will drink margaritas
lipping stale cigarettes
until the sunburn swells

and I will confide in you

this is the last of my suicides

J.P.

last call

when these lights shut off,
    i'll pretend i'm in Paris

A.S.L.

978-0-595-51226-3
0-595-51226-7

Printed in the United States
116683LV00004BA/22-78/P